WORDS *of* HOPE *and* HEALING

CHERISHING

The Art *of* Fully Living While Still Loving *and* Honoring Those Who've Died

Alan D. Wolfelt, Ph.D.

Companion
PRESS

An imprint of the Center for Loss and Life Transition | Fort Collins, Colorado

Companion Press is an imprint of the Center for Loss and Life Transition, 3735 Broken Bow Road, Fort Collins, Colorado 80526.

27   26   25   24   23   22   6   5   4   3   2   1

ISBN: 978-1-61722-320-4

CONTENTS

WELCOME

"Death ends a life, not a relationship. All the love you created
is still there. All the memories are still there."
— Morrie Schwartz

After the death of someone close to you, you enter a time of deep grief. This is a normal and necessary time of transition.

If you use this period of intense grief to actively, intentionally engage with your painful thoughts and feelings, you find ways to express them that are helpful to you. In other words, you do the hard work of mourning. You share your grief outside yourself—in doses and over time—so that you begin to integrate your loss into your ongoing life.

Essentially, you mourn well so that you can eventually go on to live well and love well. Over time, you come to understand that while your grief is not something you "get over," it has become an integrated part of your life story.

Your love is not something you "get over" either. Many people who have suffered the loss of a special loved one continue to feel their love for the person just as much after the death as they did before the death (and sometimes, even more). Is this true for you?

If it is, you may have found yourself unsure what to "do" with your love now. In fact, that is the question of this book: After your time of deep grief has passed, how do you continue to love and honor special people who have died even as you fully live out your own remaining precious days here on earth?

It's a tough question, and answering it in a way that feels right for you can be a difficult balance to find. As one grieving husband, Garrick Colwell, wrote to me, "Learning how to love my wife in her absence has been the biggest challenge I've had to face as I grieve and mourn her loss."

I am a grief counselor, educator, and author whose life's work and passion is to help grieving people and those who care for them. I've followed this calling for more than four decades now. During these years, I've had the privilege of learning from countless grievers. One of the most important things they've taught me (and that I've learned from my own personal loss experiences) is that honoring and continuing to express love for those who've gone before us is a noble, fulfilling pursuit. What's more, it's necessary. We continue to feel the love, and so we must find things to "do" with that love.

I call the practice of intentionally honoring and holding dear someone who has died "cherishing." The mindset, suggestions, and rituals in this little book will help you build cherishing into your life and your regular routines, or strengthen it if you're already doing it. They will also assist you in making the most of situations in which you may feel torn, such as holidays, anniversaries, weddings, and other celebrations and life transitions, both happy and sad.

In my experience, you can live fully while still loving and honoring those people in your life who have died.

THIS IS YOUR LIFE

"Life is amazing. And then it's awful. And then it's amazing again. And in between the amazing and the awful it's ordinary and mundane and routine. Breathe in the amazing, hold on through the awful, and relax and exhale during the ordinary. That's just living heartbreaking, soul-healing, amazing, awful, ordinary life. And it's breathtakingly beautiful."

— L.R. Knost

You are the sum total of all your life experiences to date. You have lived, and you have grown. You have probably felt many joys and many losses, big and small. If you are reading this book, you may have experienced an especially difficult loss—perhaps several—and you're not sure how to carry those loves, losses, and relationships with you into your future.

As you well know, there's no getting around the fact that life is a series of transitions and losses. Anytime we gain something new, we give something else up. It's in recognition of this inconstancy of human life that we find a need for cherishing. After all, it's how your life history becomes integrated into the present. Your past is always alive in the now because it is an inextricable part of you.

One of my beliefs is that the opportunity to live out a human life is a privilege. While I may be passionate about helping others with death, grief, and loss, the lens through which I view these realities is *life*. Everything that you've experienced in your unique journey is a sacred part of your life story. The acts of cherishing outlined in this book are intended to help you honor your past while continuing to live your life into the future.

THIS IS YOUR LOVE

"Something amazing happens when we surrender and just love.
We melt into another world, a realm of power already within us.
The world changes when we change. The world softens when we
soften. The world loves us when we choose to love the world."

— Marianne Williamson

In my view, the loves of your life are the most valuable, precious parts of your life story. In many ways, love is why you are here.

What and whom have you loved most so far in your life? Consider not only people but also pets, places, activities, jobs, callings, volunteer roles, objects, and other passions. Inside the heart graphic on the next page, make a list of your loves. Then circle the ones that have been most dear to you.

Your heart is a patchwork of all the loves in your life. Some of your loves are probably still present to you. Others have come and gone. And yet others will arrive as newcomers in the months and years still ahead of you.

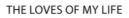

THE LOVES OF MY LIFE

_____

_____

_____

_____

_____

_____

_____

_____

_____

The loves you have lost are the pieces of your heart that along the way became torn. This is grief—the tearing of your heart. In general, the older you are, the more life losses you accumulate, and the more your heart has been touched.

When you are grieving, your grief is everything you think and feel inside of you about the loss. Grief is inner and private.

Mourning, on the other hand, is outer and visible. It is actively expressing your grief outside of yourself. And allowing yourself to mourn is critical because it is how, over time and with the support of others, you come to reconcile your grief.

To reconcile your grief is to learn to integrate it into your life. It is to acknowledge that grief has transformed, or changed you, forever. Yet, it also means to make yourself whole again by mending the parts of your heart that are torn.

Obviously, your mended, reconciled heart is never exactly the same as it was before you suffered loss. Instead, it's a patchwork heart. It's imperfect. When you poke and prod it, you can feel where the stitches are. But it's also authentic, and it's whole again.

The ongoing love you feel for someone who died—the love that invited you to pick up this book—is a big part of your patchwork heart. It's love you still feel deeply. That's how the truest loves of our lives work—they're not temporary; they're forever.

The question is, how do you live out that love when the person is no longer here beside you to receive it?

THE ART OF CHERISHING

"When I'm in cherishing mode, I'm feeling deep gratitude for the unique energy my son and daughter brought to my life. I'm generally more present to others and less focused on what I lost. Cherishing—what a powerful word."

— Patty Reis

To cherish means to protect and care for lovingly. To hold dear.

It's instinctual to want to continue to hold dear someone you love who has died. After all, they're a love of your life! They're still and always a big part of your patchwork heart. You will no doubt love them deeply for as long as you live.

You probably feel your love for the person who died constantly. You see a certain object, smell a certain scent, or go to a certain place and you are reminded of the person who was so important to you. And there it is, a reflection of your love. Your heart twinges, you may smile, you may cry. You may spend a moment feeling your love for them and missing their presence in your life.

The love naturally bubbles up, comes and goes. It's beautiful, tender, and true. And it's a kind of cherishing. But the type of cherishing I'm proposing in this book is the art of more actively engaging with the love in some way. Cherishing is intentionally creating moments—and taking advantage of opportunities when they naturally arise—in which to feel and celebrate your ongoing love more fully.

Cherishing also has to do with meaning and gratitude. When you cherish, you are honoring the relationship you had with that person and understanding how they mattered to you. You are taking pause to remember and express your appreciation.

ARE YOU READY TO CHERISH?

"In the first months after Dianne's death, I told stories of pain, tests, chemo, and ultimately last days. These stories were filled with loss and sadness. Soon I grew weary of seeing her in that way. Time offered me the opportunity to look back and recognize her depth and sparkle."

— Randy Gregg

No matter where you are in your grief journey, I imagine you often feel love for the person who died. And you might instinctively be cherishing in some of the ways we'll talk about soon.

But in my four decades of companioning people after a loss, I've found that during the intense, sharply painful early weeks and months of grief, people are generally not yet ready to actively cherish. Instead, they're naturally consumed with the need to acknowledge the reality of the death and embrace the initial pain of the loss. Yes, feelings of deep love and yearning are present, but they're still raw and reside fully within grief. They're not always ready to coexist alongside the joys and meaning of continued life.

Remembering the person who died is another early need in grief that overlaps with cherishing. This early remembering typically involves reviewing all kinds of memories, good and bad. The early work of grief is typically chaotic and all-consuming—and that's good, because that is what is necessary during that time. What I'm calling cherishing, conversely, is a longer-term way of integrating your love for someone who has died into the remainder of your days. If you're not ready for cherishing yet, that's absolutely OK. Just put this book aside and pick it up again when you are.

WHY CHERISHING IS GOOD

Building cherishing practices into your ongoing life is important because as long as the love is there inside you, it needs expression. Keeping love internalized is just like keeping any significant, ongoing emotion bottled up. Internalized emotions will often keep trying to get your attention until you give them the expression that they deserve.

One of the most fundamental truths of grief I have learned over the years is that unexpressed thoughts and feelings can weigh you down and mute your divine spark. When you carry your grief inside you without giving it voice, you open yourself to the potential of a number of long-term problems, from depression and anxiety to physical issues, relationship difficulties, addictive behaviors, and more.

The same goes for ongoing love and grief. You see, your continued feelings for and about the person who died are a big part of your life story. They are central to who you are. And if you ignore them, neglect them, underplay them, or keep them hidden, you are not being authentic.

There's a concept in psychology called "congruency." Congruency means that whatever you think and feel on the inside, that's how you act on the outside. In other words, your inner feelings and values match your outer behaviors. Incongruency means to feel and believe one way and act another.

Congruency is essential to good health—physically, cognitively, emotionally, socially, and spiritually. If you're keeping your powerful, ongoing inner love and grief completely private or a secret, on the other hand, you're being incongruent. You're not living your truth, and you're setting yourself up for those potential wellness problems I mentioned above.

One final benefit of cherishing is that it fosters mortality awareness. Acknowledging and honoring the reality of death in human life makes us better at living. We become more present and appreciative of each moment. We feel more gratitude for friends and family. We experience more awe at the beauty of nature. We revel more deeply in community. What's more, when we're more attuned to our mortality, we're more likely to slow down the pace of our lives and spend more of our precious hours and days on what really matters.

WHAT CHERISHING ISN'T

"In cherishing, I feel connected yet there is space for her to be where she is on her journey as I am on mine, even as I feel the love that nurtures our continued connection."
— Garrick Colwell

Cherishing is not living in the past while forsaking the present. It is befriending the past and acknowledging that the present "you" is a product of all your past experiences.

Cherishing is not life-denying. It is life-affirming.

Cherishing is not intentionally prolonging grief. It is acknowledging that loss is a significant part of life and that love continues.

Cherishing is not prioritizing past relationships over current relationships. It is remembering and honoring past relationships while also living and loving fully in the present.

How will you know if you're not cherishing but rather living in the past? Ask yourself if you are spending more time honoring and remembering the past than developing and strengthening current relationships and building new memories. Also consider whether or not you are engaged in your present life—appreciating each day, saying yes to chances to be with people and to experience new things, taking good care of yourself, doing things you enjoy, and finding awe and gratitude.

I don't want to give you the impression that cherishing is about staying in the past. It's not. I have seen many grievers essentially die while they are alive because they refused to actively mourn. Please, don't let this happen to you. My hope is that you will allow yourself to mourn well so you can go on to live well and love well.

HOW LONG TO CHERISH

Will there come a time when you no longer need to incorporate cherishing activities into your ongoing life? How long is too long?

As with grief and mourning in general, there is no deadline, and there are no rules. You may continue your cherishing rituals as long as you feel called to do so. If they still feel meaningful and "right" to you, that means they're still relevant and appropriate. You have a right to cherish forever.

If, on the other hand, you find that you have to force yourself (or others) to carry on a cherishing ritual after some time has passed, perhaps that's a sign to set it aside, at least for the time being. You might want to resume it later, or you might not. You can still deeply love and miss the person who died without structured rituals. Also be open to changing your cherishing rituals, adapting them for new circumstances, and trying new ones altogether.

COUNTERING CULTURAL MISCONCEPTIONS ABOUT CHERISHING

Too often our culture has it backward when it comes to grief. We tell grieving people to "put the past in the past" and "move on" before they've even begun to grasp their new reality. We encourage them to go around their grief instead of through their grief. However, when we experience grief in our lives, the truth is that we often need to go backward before we can go forward. And even when we're going forward, we still need to continue to acknowledge and honor the important experiences and loves of our past.

As you work to incorporate a good balance of cherishing into your remaining days, you may find that others will misunderstand what you're doing. Some may tell you to quit living in the past. They might suggest that your ongoing grief and love are somehow wrong. They might say that "what's done is done" and it's "time to get over it." They may prefer that you remain stoic about past losses. And they may hint that it's OK if you continue to grieve a little and quietly inside you, but you should keep it to yourself. Not only acquaintances but also your own friends and family may be among those who have never learned the importance of openly mourning and cherishing.

Yes, grief avoidance in both the short- and long-term is, broadly speaking, prominent in North America. Other cultures are better at acknowledging both the appropriateness and necessity of cherishing. They even enact group rituals to honor and stay connected with loved ones who have died. Mexico's Day of the Dead is one fairly well-known example. And on the fifteenth day of the seventh lunar month, Japanese Buddhists celebrate Obon, when it is believed that the souls of the dead revisit the living. All Soul's Day is the Catholic ritual of spending the second of November in prayer for those who have died to help them find eternal rest. And the Jewish prayers for the dead—the Kaddish—are recited every year on the anniversary of the death. In addition, in various cultures families create shrines in their homes—special altars containing memorabilia representing those who have died. They use these shrines as prominent reminders of those they have lost and as hubs for cherishing.

While I agree that the line between cherishing and living too much in the past can be blurry, the greater and more common danger is that grieving people are encouraged to keep their chins up and pretend as if their loss never happened. The best way to counter this cultural misconception is to: a) understand the value and purpose of cherishing; b) educate others about healthy mourning and cherishing; and c) invite selected people to participate in cherishing activities with you. In my experience, a little education can go a long way.

LIVING IN THE PRESENT

One final thought before we explore some suggested cherishing activities: On this day, in this moment, you are alive. While it may not always feel like it is, your aliveness is a gift. Your life has included many past experiences—and they are indeed special and part of you—but living only ever happens in the moment.

Cherishing prioritizes awareness of the present. It always recognizes that the feelings of love and loss you are experiencing are happening *right now*. Yes, you may be yearning for days gone by, but that yearning is here with you today, in this moment.

So the art of cherishing involves incorporating your ongoing feelings of love and loss into your current life. You're not pausing or escaping your current living in order to cherish. No, you're both living and cherishing at the same time.

CHERISHING AND THE SIX RECONCILIATION NEEDS

"When those you love die, the best you can do is honor their spirit for as long as you live. You make a commitment that you're going to take whatever lesson that person was trying to teach you, and you make it true to your own life... It's a positive way to keep their spirit alive in the world, by keeping it alive in yourself."

— Patrick Swayze

While grief is an intensely personal, unique experience, we must all yield to a set of basic human needs to integrate loss into our lives. I call them the six needs of mourning. As we dose ourselves with the six needs of mourning, the focus moves from the pain of the loss to the joys of the life that was lived.

1. Acknowledge the reality of the death.
2. Embrace the pain of the loss.
3. Remember the person who died.
4. Develop a new self-identity.
5. Search for meaning.
6. Let others help you—now and always.

If you're ready to work on building cherishing into your ongoing life, you've already done a lot of integrating of your early and active grief by working on these six needs. Cherishing, too, interfaces with the six needs, but in slightly different ways.

PRINCIPLES OF CHERISHING

So far we have said that cherishing is:

- Loving and holding dear
- Congruent with inner thoughts and feelings
- Active and intentional
- Present-moment-oriented
- Life-affirming
- Grateful
- Honoring of meaning
- Bittersweet (not all painful, but instead a mix of happiness and hurt)

On a more practical note, cherishing often includes the following:

- Using the name of the person who died openly, freely, and often
- Telling stories about the person who died
- Making others feel comfortable and invited to talk about the person who died

- Offering others reminders of the person who died when appropriate (e.g., "Today was your grandpa's birthday," or "She loved eating ice cream."
- Keeping photos and objects that remind you of the person who died on display and talking about them with others
- Marking special days by honoring or "including" the person who died in some way (more about this soon)

DOSING YOUR CHERISHING

Like active early mourning, cherishing isn't something you can "accomplish" all at once. It's more an occasional and forever practice.

So think of cherishing as something you do in small doses—little bits here and there. Your doses of cherishing might be regular—for example, something you do on certain special days—or they might be irregular and spontaneous—something you do at those times when you feel most pulled to love and remember.

WHEN TO CHERISH

There are no real rules about cherishing, just the general framework I've been talking about in this book. But here are some thoughts about appropriate times for cherishing.

Spontaneously

You may feel the call to cherish spontaneously, on any given day at any given time. You might wake up one Saturday and think, "I'm feeling my love for _____ this morning, so I'm going to spend some time today cherishing them." Or you might be talking to someone and suddenly feel compelled to share a special anecdote or memory. My only advice about informal, spur-of-the-moment cherishing is this: Do it! It's good for your soul.

On special days

In addition to saying "yes" to spontaneous cherishing moments, you will probably find that planning ahead for some cherishing opportunities will help certain moments feel more integrated and meaningful. Cherishing can be a ritualized activity carried out on special days such as birthdays, anniversaries, holidays, and family occasions like weddings, reunions, etc.

For example, the McPheters family shared with me that on special days they often find meaningful ways to remember their daughter Brooke, who died at age 15. On what would have been Brooke's 21st birthday, they took her friends to Las Vegas for several days filled with fun and adventure. Last year on her birthday they sponsored an Easter egg hunt in their community in her name.

Triggers

Certain places, songs, smells, and other triggers can cause memories and feelings of love and loss to suddenly come rushing in. I call these experiences "griefbursts." When this happens, you can choose to stop whatever it is you're doing for a few minutes and pause for some intentional cherishing.

In my case, my father loved spaghetti. Whenever I am at the grocery store and go down the pasta aisle, I find myself taking pause to remember my dad and allow whatever feelings that come up to be experienced.

Regardless of when and how you cherish, remember to cherish in doses and seek to find a balance of fully living in the present and cherishing that works for you.

Cherishing alone or together

It often feels natural to cherish in the quiet of our own hearts or to carry out personal, private cherishing rituals. These are indeed profoundly loving and congruent practices. But I also encourage you to add some cherishing rituals where you can invite others to be a part of the experiences. Many of the example rituals on pages 32 to 48 can be adapted for use by a pair, a family, or a larger group.

Group cherishing acknowledges that the precious people who died were part of a community. You loved them, but no doubt so did others. These other mourners, too, would benefit from the healing balm of cherishing rituals. What's more, these shared mourning activities strengthen bonds among the living. Holding a group cherishing ritual annually, perhaps on a birthday or anniversary of a death, is one way to do this. I know families who regularly hold fun runs, fundraisers, and vigils. Another way to do this is to insert a brief cherishing ritual into established family holiday traditions such as lighting a candle in memory of a loved one who died.

Conversely, you may find that some friends and family members are hesitant about or reluctant to participate in cherishing rituals. Due to culturally conditioned grief avoidance, they might suggest that group cherishing activities only serve to "dredge up the past" or "open old wounds." They may also feel uncertain about what it will be like to mourn openly in the presence of others long after the funeral. While you shouldn't force others to participate, you can educate them about the human need for regular remembrance and the celebratory gratitude of cherishing. If some are judging the appropriateness of your cherishing rituals, it can be very appropriate to exclude them. Hesitant participants may express doubts or question the significance of your rituals, which can ruin them for those who do find meaning and value in these activities.

Also, keep in mind that group rituals can commemorate many people who have died. If you coordinate a cherishing event with multiple friends, for example, each of you can honor whoever you'd like as part of the activity. Or if you're doing a family cherishing ritual, you can remember any number of family members and/or close friends who have gone before you. One thing to consider is the possibility of inviting people who may not have known the person who died to join you in the cherishing activity. After all, they still may want to be of support to you, and you may find comfort in their presence.

WHAT ARE RITUALS?

In the next section of this book, I will be presenting a number of example cherishing rituals. But what do I mean by "ritual"? I simply mean actions that we perform in a certain way and in a certain sequence for a purpose that has emotional and spiritual meaning and is greater than the sum of its parts.

These rituals aren't formal ceremonies (although you could adapt some of them for use in more formal ceremonies). In fact, most of them can be brief, informal, and simple. They can be performed alone or in groups. They honor ongoing love and grief deeply yet simply.

Here are the ingredients that turn an informal moment of remembering and grieving into a cherishing ritual:

INTENTIONALITY
Take a few seconds at the beginning of each ritual to speak your intention—in other words, state what you intend to gain or

reinforce from the activity. For example, "the purpose of this ritual is to honor and remember what grandpa brought to the dance of our lives."

ACTIONS
Rituals always involve your body. Moving or using your body in certain ways as you perform a ritual helps integrate your physical, cognitive, emotional, social and spiritual selves. Examples include lighting a candle, holding your body in a certain posture, bowing your head, standing in a certain spot, moving from point A to point B to point C, etc.

SYMBOLISM
Symbols are significant elements of ritual. Objects important to your story of loss and ongoing love can be powerful touchstones in your cherishing rituals. These are often linking objects (see page 45) but can also be spiritual symbols, flowers, candles, and more.

SEQUENCE
Rituals have a beginning, middle, and end. The parts of the ritual are usually performed in a certain order because the sequence itself builds meaning and effectiveness.

PRESENCE
Rituals stand apart from the rest of our days. We don't allow the busy-ness of our lives to intrude on them. Instead, we create a time and place, and we commit to being fully present physically, cognitively, emotionally, socially, and spiritually as we carry out the ritual.

HEART

Rituals are emotional. In cherishing rituals, we commit to being open to and accepting of whatever emotions arise. We allow ourselves the gifts of time and presence to acknowledge, welcome, and feel our feelings, no matter what they are.

SPIRIT

The spiritual nature of ritual is what creates the transformative power of the experience. On the surface, we may seem to be carrying out a series of simple, no-big-deal actions. But with the addition of intention, symbolism, intention, presence, and heart, we are elevating the experience into the realm of the spiritual. Even when a cherishing ritual doesn't seem explicitly spiritual, it's spiritual.

These ingredients can be manifested and combined in infinite ways as you create and carry out cherishing rituals that feel meaningful to you, your family, and community. Consider including bits of music, readings, prayers or poetry, moments of silence, moments of sharing, linking objects, and other ritual elements. Again, your rituals don't need to be elaborate or lengthy, but making them special in just one or two ways will elevate them into experiences that feel worthy of your gratitude and continuing love for those who have died.

THE SIX OPPORTUNITIES
OF CHERISHING

*"Cherish your friends and family as if your life
depended on it. Because it does."*

— Ann Richards

What I'm calling the "six opportunities of cherishing" are extensions of the six needs of mourning. These activities can help you cherish well as you continue to live and love fully. The examples below are opportunities to cherish in depth and with structure.

As you carry out these activities, keep in mind that the opportunities are not mutually exclusive. For example, you could be cherishing your stories of love and loss while at the same time cherishing who you are, both past and present.

You will note there is space provided after each opportunity to document any specific ideas that may work best for you.

1. THE OPPORTUNITY TO CHERISH YOUR STORIES OF LOVE AND LOSS

In active grief, you worked through acknowledging the reality of the death in both your head and in your heart. Part of this step was telling yourself and others the stories of the person's life, death, and your relationship with them, often over and over again. The more you thought about and told the stories, the more deeply you were able to acknowledge the reality and finality of the death.

Now, as you move into cherishing, you are ready to take these more integrated stories of love and loss and prepare yourself to honor and celebrate them.

EXAMPLE CHERISHING RITUALS

- Write down stories of the person's life, death, and your love and loss. You can select to read one aloud at special holiday times, such as before Thanksgiving dinner. Or compile the stories into a book you have printed and give copies of the book to family and friends.

- Create or purchase a plaque or framed saying that sums up some of how you feel about the person who died. Hang it somewhere prominent, and consider using it in a daily private ritual, such as standing in front of it for a minute each morning as you set your intention for the day and affirm your love. This would also work with a special photo of the person who died. For example, I have a framed photo of my father in his backyard by a cherry tree. Under the photo I have listed some of his favorite sayings I heard him say time and time again, such as "When you leave a room, turn out the lights!"

- Make a piece of art that represents your relationship with the person who died and display it in your home. Whenever an appropriate opportunity arises, you can explain the art and its significance to visitors.

- Make a ritual of visiting the grave, scattering site, or another special place you associate with the person who died. When you're there, consider stepping through a ritual of visitation. This can be anything you want as long as it's a series of steps you follow each time. For example, you might always bring fresh flowers and a picnic blanket. You might sit down and talk aloud to the person who died, updating them on everything that's happened since your last visit. You might read them something you've written or a poem by someone else, sing them a song, or play music on an instrument or simply on your phone. Consider closing your visitation ritual in some way, such as with a prayer or affirmation.

- Patty Reis wears a bracelet every day inscribed with the handwriting of her precious daughter who died. The message says, "Well done good and faithful servant." To Patty, the handwriting is evidence of Karen and the life she lived.

_____

_____

_____

_____

2. THE OPPORTUNITY TO CHERISH YOUR PAIN (BECAUSE IT'S YOUR LOVE)

Whenever you feel a pang of grief, welcome its presence because it is your forever love for the person who died. I sometimes think that these normal, necessary griefbursts are simply the people who have died reminding us not to forget them.

Cherishing your ongoing love is naturally bittersweet. I call it "sappiness"—that poignant blend of happiness and sadness that often makes us smile, laugh, and cry at the same time. But the alternative is to stop loving the person who died, and who would ever choose that?

EXAMPLE CHERISHING RITUALS

- Make or write out a Valentine each year for the person who died and leave it somewhere appropriate, such as the grave or scattering site. It can also be dropped into a mail slot with the address as "heaven" or something similar.

- Create an anniversary ritual. On the anniversary of the death or another special date that you know will be painful for you, set up a routine for yourself that allows you to take a few moments to focus on and embrace your pain, your love, and your gratitude. The ritual can be done individually or with a group.

- Intentionally choose a song that speaks to both your pain and your love. Whenever you are feeling your pain, stop what you are doing, put on your headphones, and listen to the song. Cry if you feel like crying. Then tell someone else about your song ritual and how it helps you cherish the person who died. My father enjoyed Frank Sinatra and Big Band music like Glenn Miller and Tommy Dorsey. When I want to cherish my dad, I play some of this music and embrace my ongoing love for him.

• Find purpose through engaging in a meaningful activity. Engage yourself with an activity, organization, or volunteer effort that you associate with the person who died. As you do the activity, wear or carry something that reminds you of your special person. Tell someone else at the activity about the person who died and how this activity helps you cherish them.

Brian Dagle died by suicide at the age of 19. After his death, the family poured their love for him into the Brian Dagle Foundation and Brian's Healing Hearts Center for Hope & Healing, located in Niantic, Connecticut. Their mission is dedicated to the healing of grieving adults as well as community education on suicide prevention and awareness. In addition to sponsoring community events, the foundation runs support groups for various types of losses. They also put on regular educational programs on grief and spirituality.

- On the anniversary of the sudden passing of her husband, Carolyn Williams held an informal ceremony with friends and family. John had died unexpectedly at the age of 57. At the ceremony Carolyn passed out small pieces of paper and asked those who knew John to write down what they wished they could have said to him before he died. Everyone spent a few minutes writing a note to John, then one by one, the participants dropped their notes into a vase of water. The paper was water-soluble, and each note dissolved almost immediately. This opportunity to express themselves about what they wished they would have been able to say to John proved to be an excellent opportunity to cherish his place in their lives.

Your meaningful cherishing activity can be small or large, intermittent or regular. Simply do what feels right for you. Notice how you feel during and after the activity.

_____

_____

_____

_____

_____

_____

_____

3. THE OPPORTUNITY TO CHERISH YOUR MEMORIES

I hope you have many good memories of the person who died, but whether you have a lot or a few, you have so many opportunities for cherishing them.

The memories you have of this person are as unique as your relationship was with them. Therefore, you might want to capture them in a more permanent fashion. In this way, the person you have loved continues to live on in your family for years into the future.

EXAMPLE CHERISHING RITUALS

- Assemble a photo album that captures the person's life as well as their unique personality and interests. Choose some of your favorite photos. Consider adding captions with dates, places, and other helpful information. If others might be interested or have photos to contribute, this would be an ideal group activity.

- If you have access to video footage of the person who died, you can make a movie of the person's life. If you don't have the computer skills to do this yourself, consider asking someone to assist you.

- On special days such as the person's birthday or anniversary of their death, share a memory on social media (on your pages and/or the person's memorialized accounts) and invite others who knew the person to do the same.

- On special days such as holidays, text or email a brief memory to your group of contacts who also cared about the person who died. Consider making the anecdote pertinent to the holiday or time of year.

- Make a gratitude jar. Whenever you remember something about the person who died that makes you feel grateful, jot it down on a slip of paper and put it in the gratitude jar. Invite friends and family members to do the same. Once a year, at a group event such as a birthday or on the anniversary of the death, gather everyone together and read the slips of paper aloud. Nan Zastrow's family still does this in memory of their son, Chad, who died many years ago. "It feels good to remember with some kind of ritual," she says.

_____

_____

_____

_____

_____

_____

_____

4. THE OPPORTUNITY TO CHERISH WHO YOU ARE, PAST AND PRESENT

You love someone who died, and they in turn loved you. What did they love about you then? What would they love about you today if they could see you now? Cherishing yourself through the eyes of the person who died is an important aspect of your cherishing practices. After all, love is a two-way street, and in their absence, you are called upon to love yourself on their behalf.

I strongly believe that living the best life you can, and being the best person you can be, fulfills this aspect of cherishing. You are still here. What will you do to make the person who died proud? And how will you choose to live out the privilege of still being alive?

EXAMPLE CHERISHING RITUALS

- In the form of a letter you write on a certain day each year, tell the person who died how you are taking care of yourself and living and loving well recently. Update them on things you know they would like to hear about. Share your struggles and challenges, too, but look for ways to be proud of yourself on their behalf. If you're not a letter writer, you can speak these updates to them at their gravesite or any special place you associate with them.

- Include the person who died in any future rituals that honor you or your family members. For example, if you will be receiving an honor at work, mention them in your remarks. Or if you or someone in your family will be getting married, graduating, retiring, etc., find a way to incorporate the spirit of the person who died into the ceremonies.

- Schedule self-care activities that honor the person's love for you. At the beginning of each year or each quarter, spend some time making a list of all the self-cherishing activities you may be participating in. Include both necessary tasks (such as medical check-ups) and fun items (such as weekend getaways). Then take steps to actually schedule and commit to each of these activities.

Use what you've learned about death, grief, and mourning to be your most authentic self as often as possible. Take the time and make the effort to tell others how much they mean to you. Say yes to opportunities to do what you feel called to do. Celebrate your life each day, and in doing so, you will be living on behalf of the person who died and cherishing their memory.

_____

_____

_____

_____

_____

_____

5. THE OPPORTUNITY TO CHERISH YOUR FEELINGS OF MEANING AND PURPOSE (PAST AND PRESENT)

In your past, what has given your life a sense of meaning and purpose? What does so today?

When someone loved dies, it's normal for feelings of meaning and purpose to be questioned. But over time, as you mourned actively and worked toward reconciliation, you have probably taken big steps toward regaining and recreating a sense of meaning and purpose in your life.

Now you have the opportunity to cherish your past, your present, and your future aspects of meaning and purpose in your life. All are part of your life story. All are part of your patchwork heart. And all may intertwine with the life you shared with the person who died.

In fact, I believe that after someone we love dies, we have a responsibility to live forward not only for ourselves but also for them. They live on through us, in our deeds and actions. We have the opportunity to further any of their unfinished work and to realize any of their unfinished dreams. We also have the opportunity to work toward becoming the best versions of ourselves as we live our lives passionately and in service to others.

EXAMPLE CHERISHING RITUALS

- Support a cause that's related in some meaningful way to the person who died. Your time, talents, and resources can go a long way toward making a difference in the lives of others. If the person who died was passionate about a certain activity or cause, supporting that cause is a way of cherishing.

One way that Shanna and Gary McPheters honor their daughter Brooke, who was killed by a drunk driver, is by regular volunteering for various organizations related to this issue. These include organizations such as REDDI (Report Every Drunk Driver Immediately) and their local Citizens Academy program offered by their police department.

• Make mementos of the person's belongings. Rather than donating or disposing of the clothing and other belongings of the person who died, consider saving some of these items for possible future use. It can be very meaningful to pass along an object when an appropriate opportunity arises. For example, you might not need or want your brother's camping gear. But because camping was a special activity to him, you may find meaning in providing some of his items to someone who also enjoys similar pursuits.

In addition, things such as quilts, throw pillows, and stuffed animals can be made from the fabric of the clothing that belonged to the person who died. These often make truly meaningful, irreplaceable gifts to others who also loved the person.

I find meaning and purpose in wearing my father's 1945 Bulova watch. It was given to him by my grandmother on the day that he graduated from high school. Whenever I have it on, I feel a special closeness to him.

• Plan a road trip. Create an itinerary of places that have been meaningful to you, your family, and the person who died. As you visit each special spot, take time to reflect and remember. If you keep a travel journal along the way, you'll have a valuable keepsake you can reread in the years to come.

_____

_____

_____

_____

_____

6. THE OPPORTUNITY TO CHERISH YOUR RELATIONSHIPS WITH OTHERS (PAST AND PRESENT)

Love and relationships—if you ask me, that's the meaning of life. Oh sure, along the way we encounter the full range of human emotions and experiences. And besides our attachments, there are other parts that bring us joy. Spending time in nature, traveling, learning new skills, enjoying good food and drink, participating in spiritual practices—if you took love out of the equation, all of these things and more could still make our lives interesting and enjoyable.

But would our lives have deep meaning if we didn't also love others and receive love in return? I don't think so.

I would suggest that in your patchwork heart, your most significant relationships with others occupy the largest patches. Remembering and honoring those relationships, both past and present, is central to any cherishing moment, activity, or ritual.

Even as we cherish those who have died, we are well-served to remind ourselves that it is also critically important to cherish our relationships with those who are still alive. Relationships require three nutrients to thrive: proximity, repetition, and quality time. In short, this means often spending quality time in close contact with the people you care about.

This may sound overly obvious, but when we're physically near someone frequently, we're more likely to develop a strong relationship with them. Being together in person is best, but when that's not possible—such as when people are separated by distance—it's still possible to maintain strong ties through frequent video calls, emails, and texts.

But quality time is the other essential factor here. As you may have experienced yourself, you can be around someone every day but not feel close to them. No, emotional bonds are built on quality interaction, which is time spent with another person or people in which you are focusing on each other, communicating well, empathizing, and truly sharing an experience.

Cherishing past relationships works much in the same way:

• *Promixity*
Those who have died can no longer be physically present to us. For many people in grief, this is the hardest reality to embrace. But you can still feel physically close to them by cherishing linking objects, which are special belongings and mementos of the person who died. Visiting the burial or scattering site is another way. Spending time in locations that were meaningful to the person who died or to your relationship can also foster that feeling of proximity. And finally, for some people, being in a spiritual place (such as the "thin places" I talk about on page 46) can evoke strong feelings of connection with your loved one.

• *Repetition*
Cherishing often but in brief little doses is a good way to maintain bonds with those who have died. Simply mentioning aloud the person's name whenever you think of them is one good way. For me, at times when I see an extraordinary sunrise or sunset, I'm called to cherish my parents and reflect on everything I learned from them.

• *Quality time*

This, I think, is where the need for rituals of cherishing comes in. I've given a number of examples of cherishing rituals already and will provide several more in the pages to come. I remind you that while moments of spontaneous, informal cherishing are precious, more structured cherishing rituals that combine elements such as intention, actions, symbolism, sequence, heart, and spirit can result in cherishing experience that are memorable and meaningful.

EXAMPLE CHERISHING RITUALS

• Cherish in a thin place. In the Celtic tradition, "thin places" are spots where the separation between the physical world and the spiritual world seem tenuous. They are places where the veil between heaven and earth, between the holy and the everyday, are so thin that when we are near them, we intuitively sense the spiritual world and often feel closer to those who have died. Thin places may be places of worship or sacred sites but are often outdoors, in nature, commonly where water and land meet or land and sky come together. Ultimately, all that matters is that a place feels "thin" to you.

• Keep up a tradition that was important to the person who died. If the person you miss was especially fond of a certain ritual or tradition—perhaps something on a holiday or other certain time of year—you can honor and "include" them in your ongoing life by continuing the tradition. For example, my father always enjoyed the carving of the turkey at Thanksgiving. In my family, before we have dinner we have a tradition of always pausing for a few moments of silence and remembering him.

- Throw a party. One of the ways Becky Torres carries forward her love for her daughter, Brooke, is by holding what she calls "heavenly birthday dinner parties" for friends and family. She always serves Brooke's favorite pink-champagne cake from a local bakery.

  Likewise, Garrick Colwell invites friends and family to gather on Zoom for an hour each year on the date of the death of his wife, Kinsloe. They catch up with one another as they share stories, memories, and photos.

- Hold a candle-lighting ceremony. Gather people together in a circle. Pass out candles to everyone. To start: light your candle and say, "We are here today to honor our love and memories, which never die. Our love for _____ is a flame we carry inside of each of us." Then share something you love and miss about the person who died. Then invite the person next to you to do the same. Continue around the circle until everyone has shared. At the end, consider closing the ceremony with a brief reading or an appropriate piece of music.

- Dedicate something to the person who died. This could be a park bench, a newly planted tree, a scholarship, or anything you want. Gather a small group or a large one. Talk to the guests about what is being dedicated and why. Invite them to participate in the ritual in some way. Close with a short reading or prayer.

• Support others in grief. If you're reading this book, you may well be someone who is interested in helping other people who have suffered life losses. When you feel the time is right for you, you might explore ways to help others in grief. For example, volunteering as a support group facilitator or providing companionship to a fellow mourner. These are cherishing activities because you will be using your love for the person who died as motivation to help others who are grieving.

_____

_____

_____

_____

_____

CHERISHING AS A WAY OF LIFE

"Cherishing creates a shift. Instead of measuring, comparing,
weighing, and competing with people, we savor them.
We hold them close. We look more carefully.
We listen more deeply. Until we cherish our life, and
everyone else's life, we will never find our way home."

— Randy Gregg

Cherishing isn't just a way of remembering, honoring, and continuing to love someone who has died. It can also be a way of being. Do you cherish each new day and every encounter with the people you care about? Do you routinely place your attention on what matters? And conversely, are you able to shrug off or ignore the small stuff?

Grief cherishing makes you better at life cherishing. The more you actively engage in cherishing someone who has died, the more you may find your patchwork heart opening, making you a more kind, compassionate, and helpful person. It's as if the act of cherishing unlocks your vulnerability and capacity for empathy. It better attunes you to emotionality and spirituality.

The spiritual guru Ram Dass was talking about this when he suggested that we should cherish one another and ourselves in the same way that we appreciate trees:

> *When you go out into the woods, and you look at the trees, you see all these different trees. And some of them are bent, and some of them are straight, and some of them are evergreens, and some of them are whatever. And you look at the tree and you allow it. You see why it is the way it is. You sort of understand that it didn't get enough light, and so it turned that way. You appreciate the tree.*
>
> *The minute you get near humans, you lose all that. And you are constantly saying, "You are too this, or I'm too this." That judgment mind comes in. And so I practice turning people into trees. Which means appreciating them just as they are.*

"Since Kinsloe died," Garrick Colwell wrote to me, "I have set out to live from a deeper place within my heart than the day before. I strive to be kind, compassionate, and graceful in the ways I love, behave, and interact with others. This is my way of honoring her and finding meaning in her life."

Garrick's right. Cherishing is more than a way of living in the now—it is a way of loving in the now. When you combine those two practices—the art of mindful presence and the art of cherishing—you have a recipe for human life that savors every drop of beauty and meaning.

But I realize that cherishing isn't all good, either. Life changes still befall us all the time, and they're often not changes we'd choose. Losses stack one atop the next. Yet when we encounter these changes and losses from a position of cherishing, we are better prepared to embrace them for what they are—unavoidable parts of being human.

A FINAL WORD

*"You would think that the cherishing activities
I do would make me sad, but cherishing Brooke and all the
memories brings me so much joy."*
— Becky Torres

To cherish is to celebrate and honor love, which is the
greatest gift of human life. Grief is love, and love is grief.
They are two sides of the same precious coin, and we find
meaning in cherishing both.

I hope you have found this exploration of cherishing in
ongoing grief to be of help to you. I hope you will consider
sending me your cherishing stories and reflections. I invite
you to email me at drwolfelt@centerforloss.com.

Right now, close your eyes, open your heart, and remember
the smile of the person who died. As this memory twinges
your patchwork heart, take a moment to cherish the love
and loss you feel. Express your gratitude, then consider how
you will carry this love forward into the rest of your life,
your living, and your loving.

YOUR NOTES ON CHERISHING

YOUR NOTES ON CHERISHING

_____

_____

_____

_____

_____

_____

_____

_____

_____

_____

_____

_____

_____

_____

_____

_____

_____

_____

_____

_____

_____

_____

ABOUT THE AUTHOR

Alan D. Wolfelt, Ph.D., is a respected author and educator on the topics of companioning others and healing in grief. He serves as Director of the Center for Loss and Life Transition and is on the faculty at the University of Colorado Medical

School's Department of Family Medicine. Dr. Wolfelt has written many bestselling books on healing in grief, including *Understanding Your Grief, Healing Your Grieving Heart*, and *Grief One Day at a Time*. Visit www.centerforloss.com to learn more about grief and loss and to order Dr. Wolfelt's books.

The Hope and Healing Series
Concise books of wisdom and comfort

Readers and counselors often ask Dr. Wolfelt to write books on specialized topics not well-covered elsewhere in the grief literature. He created the Hope and Healing Series to fulfill their requests. These short books focus in on particular types of loss and aspects of grief that while distinct, are not uncommon. They affect many millions of people worldwide, each of whom deserves affirmation, support, and guidance for their unique circumstances.

All Dr. Wolfelt's publications can be ordered by mail from:
Companion Press, 3735 Broken Bow Road, Fort Collins, CO 80526
(970) 226-6050 • www.centerforloss.com